The Scholar, As The True Progressive And Conservative: Illustrated In The Life Of Hugo Grotius, And By The Law Of Nations

Samuel Sullivan Cox

In the interest of creating a more extensive selection of rare historical book reprints, we have chosen to reproduce this title even though it may possibly have occasional imperfections such as missing and blurred pages, missing text, poor pictures, markings, dark backgrounds and other reproduction issues beyond our control. Because this work is culturally important, we have made it available as a part of our commitment to protecting, preserving and promoting the world's literature. Thank you for your understanding.

THE SCHOLAR,

AS THE TRUE

PROGRESSIVE AND CONSERVATIVE:

ILLUSTRATED IN THE LIFE OF

HUGO GROTIUS,

And by the Law of Nations.

AN ADDRESS,

Delivered before the Athenian Literary Society of the Ohio University,
August 3, 1852.

BY

SAMUEL S. COX.

COLUMBUS:
PRINTED BY SCOTT & BASCOM.
1852.

CORRESPONDENCE.

ATHENIAN HALL,
August 5th, 1852.

S. S. COX, ESQ.:

DEAR SIR,—
In compliance with a duty imposed upon us by the Athenian Literary Society, we embrace this early opportunity to express to you, on behalf of the Society, their highest satisfaction for your able and highly gratifying Address, delivered to them at their former request, and would respectfully invite you to furnish them with a copy of the same for publication.

SAML. MUTCHMORE,
SARDINE P. REED,   } *Committee.*
P. B. STANBERY,

ATHENS, *August 5,* 1852.

GENTLEMEN:
My manuscript is at your disposal. Would it were more worthy of the subject, the commendation you bestow, and your Society, which has honored me with its attention.

Sincerely,

SAM'L S. COX.

SAML. MUTCHMORE,
SARDINE P. REED,   } Committee.
P. B. STANBERY,

THE SCHOLAR,

THE TRUE PROGRESSIVE AND CONSERVATIVE:

As Illustrated in the Life of Hugo Grotius, and by the Law of Nations.

THOUGHT only is permanent. Power, physical and personal, unaccompanied by reflection, is fruitless and ignoble. Thought has an eternal pulsation in the human soul. Fainter or stronger, waking or sleeping, it still indicates that life burns in the bosom of man. So long as that life burns, so long will Thought progress, and lead in its train the happiness and glory of human nature.

And as, without Progress, decay is sure; as Progress is the only Conservator of that which is useful, fair and good; and as the scholar or the thinker is the vein in which this active principle must bound and beat, he becomes the true Conservative and Progressive. The world owes to him what it has; for he has treasured up to a life beyond life, and hallowed by the lights of history and poetry, the spiritual results of Time. It has measured and will measure its advancement by his influence; for he gives the impulse and projects the theory, although others may consummate. The sheaves, which now make our fields placers of more than Californian richness, were once but seed; and past deeds of high emprize and signal worth, were once silently sown in the fallow ground of Thought. The ages of the world were long polar nights, before Greece impearled their memories. The only glimmer in the middle ages, burned in the cloister of the monkish scholar and in the bright eye of the Arabic Nomad. The civilization which dawned in the fifteenth century, followed the destruction of Byzantium and the dispersion of her Greek literature and scholars.

My theme is the Scholar, as the true Conservative and Progressive, illustrated in the life of HUGO GROTIUS, a scholar of Holland, and the architect of our International Law.

It was for a long time a problem whether man progressed. Until the latter part of the sixteenth century, motion was taken for movement; marking time for the forward march. Then, a number of gifted men, instinct with the idea that the world was not finished, began to note the intellectual phenomena of their era, and found in its stagnancy a motive to reform. Originality of thought and experiment took the place of logomachy and Aristotle. Lilly and Scotus ceased their intellectual sparring and fencing, and Bacon and his compeers entered and drove the schoolmen from the arena. From this time may be dated, and to this may be ascribed many, if not the most, of the improvements in the arts of life and in the sciences, which are ours to-day.

There is no truer test of a great man, than his quick perception of the needs of our intellectual nature, and his ready supply of the plan for its culture. Bacon stands this test eminently. In 1626, he yielded up that spirit which had dedicated its last years to the "Instauration." He had taught the world, that belief should not rest upon mere speculation; that theories, however harmonious, should not be framed and facts supposed to follow them necessarily, but that general laws should spring from actual facts; so that when from such a collection of facts laws were deduced, they should be so applied as to give confirmation and lead to new laws.

But Bacon did little to illustrate his own principles by experiment. His contemporaries, however, as if moved by his own great impulse, began the work of progress. Kepler published his Harmonice Mundi, at the same time that Bacon was repolishing his "Instauration." While Richelieu was receiving the Cardinal's hat from the King of France at Lyons; while Gustavus Adolphus was hurling his thunderbolts of war from the North; while Shakspeare was writing plays and performing them at the Globe theatre, and John Hampden was canvassing for his first seat in Parliament, and preparing for that contest between royal presumption and popular privilege which concluded with the Commonwealth and Cromwell; while Philip II. was warring against Holland for the mastery, and Adventure was roaming the western seas to plant the standards of Spain and England on unknown shores;—while these influences were developing diplomatic finesse and mere national politics, and amidst this general inquiry of genius and increase of science, there was another and a more noble revolution, noiselessly wrought by the patient pen of an humble student of Holland.

His name was HUGO GROTIUS. His revolution was not destructive, but constructive. By collecting the world's moral sense and distilling it through his own heart and conscience; by searching the best authorities of ancient learning and interpreting the will of God as revealed in his written word; by collecting the customs, treaties and statutes common to civilized nations, and in this inductive mode illustrating the principles which Bacon was then publishing—and, it is said, even under the exhortation of Bacon himself—he gave life to that universal code which pervades the nations, as gravity does the stars by its invisible bonds!

I trust that it may not seem inappropriate to illustrate a scholar's worth and to weigh his influence upon the world, in a sphere to which recent events in this country and in Europe, have given such an intensity of interest.

The growing importance of our own Union in the world—its either arm resting upon the sea—its place midway between the slothful millions of the Orient and the stirring masses of Europe, drawing the German and Irish from the one side, and even the Coolies from their hermitage of exclusiveness, upon the other; its emigration overteeming its native growth; its plain, unmistakable position before the world, as the exponent of ideas which would forever crush the odious distinctions of caste and nobility, and the slavish creeds of king-craft—admonish us that the theme is one upon which our time may be richly employed. What is the limit of our connection with despotisms and monarchies? How far may these over-ride the interests of the people and inhumanly imprison for political offences? Where is the point for our recognition of popular commotions, our protest, or our arms? What is the basis and sanction of our law international, and what is its executive? All these questions prompt us to examine heedfully the mission of young DE GROOT, from which this impalpable agency received its first well-directed force.

In turning over the pages of history, during the latter part of the sixteenth century, the eyes of few would fall upon the name of GROTIUS. The cursory eye would seek as vainly for an eminence in the flat marshes of Holland, as the mind for greatness among her children. Arms and theologic strife—that bloody tournament between Christian powers, known as the Thirty Years' War—diplomacy and balancings of power, detain and distract the attention; yet in the son of the curator of the college at Leyden, was then and there implanted a germ, which expanded with his years, whose grateful influence overspread the nations and sheltered them in fraternal sympathies.

He was born at Delft, in Holland, not far from the Hague, in 1583. His father was a lawyer and a poet of some reputation. The time and scene of his entrance upon life, was congenial to his active mind. The states of Holland were then at the summit of their prosperity. They formed a confederation of Republics, instinct with a boldness and pervaded by an industry not unlike our own. Freedom inspired them with that enterprize, which sent fleets to the West for discovery, and argosies to the Indies for commerce.* They contended triumphantly with Spain, and suc-

---

* "The United Provinces were soon without any rival on the seas. In Europe alone they had 1200 merchant-ships in activity, and upwards of 70,000 sailors constantly employed. They built annually 2000 vessels. In the year 1598, eighty

cessfully with England for maritime glory. They were true countrymen of the ancient mynheers of Manhattan, who resisted the encroachments of the King of England upon their provincial privileges, and of those gallant men who, at the siege of Antwerp and Leyden, tore away their dykes—the result of long years of persevering labor—and gave their land to the dominion of the free waves of ocean, rather than suffer it to render fealty to the haughty Spaniard, and themselves to be his serfs.* They were akin to the brave Admiral who, in 1653, swept the channel with his broom; and to that Prince of Orange, who, in 1688, left his native land, to establish for Englishmen those charters and petitions of right upon which the Stuarts had trampled, and upon which our own Revolution was founded. Companioned with Freedom and with perfect liberty of the press and of speech—rare privileges then—and under such influences, the mind of Grotius was developed. They had much to do with giving it that denationalization, which was so essential for one whose Reason would become authority to settle the vexed questions of his time, and the quarrels of mankind, forever. He surveyed no people with partial eye. No Alpine boundary inclosed,—no classic heritage of national glory discolored,—and no Rhine or Tweed, Danube or Scheldt, limited his view of human interests. The lowlands

---

ships sailed from their ports for the Indies or America. They carried on, besides, an extensive trade on the coast of Guinea, whence they brought large quantities of gold-dust; and found, in short, in all quarters of the globe the reward of their skill, industry, and courage."—*Grattan's History of the Netherlands, p.* 175.

* The historian from whom the above annotation was made, after describing the contests, in 1585, between the forces of Holland—which amounted but to 5500 men, under Maurice of Nassau—and the troops of the Prince of Parma, amounting to 80,000, gives a stirring account of the stupendous siege of Antwerp. "The river Scheldt was closed up. Infernal machines and fire-ships were sent against the bridge and fleets of the Spaniard, carrying terrible destruction; but all in vain. The beleaguered town received no relief. One last resource was left —that which had formerly been resorted to at Leyden, and by which the place was saved. To enable them to inundate the immense plain which stretched between Lillo and Strabrock up to the walls of Antwerp, it was necessary to cut through the dyke which defended it against the irruptions of the Eastern Scheldt."

of Holland, where the sea once had no limits, the rivers no beds or banks, the earth no solidity, early reclaimed by the unromantic dyke from the slime of the Ocean, was a landscape whose features, unrelieved by its multitudes of wind-mills, were not calculated to endear themselves to his memory. The waves of the sea—that common which no man could parcel or inclose—were ever ebbing and flowing at his door, emblematic of those rights common to humanity upon her bosom.*

As a boy at school, Grotius was precocious, with a precocity that withered not with age, nor grew stale by custom. At the age of nine, he made extemporaneous Latin verses. At the age of fifteen, he published his edition of Martian Capella, a prodigy of youthful learning, and disputed publicly in the schools of philosophy and civil law. His memory was so astonishing, that he is said to have remembered the names of a regiment, after having heard the muster-roll once called. When fifteen, he had read the pages of Cicero, Apuleius, Albericus, Aquila, Porphyry, Aristotle, Strabo, Ptolemy, Pliny and Euclid, and was accounted so wonderful an instance of early acquirements, that a contemporary remarked: "The last man has at length arrived. The man Grotius is born!" From this time, he was each year prompted to some new work. Inspired by the ambition, *a laudatis laudari*, he pursued the rigid study of the law, which, unless too sedulously pursued, to the neglect of more generous studies, does more to

---

* Pliny, the Naturalist, has left us a picture of its state in his days. "There the ocean pours in his flood every day, and produces a perpetual uncertainty whether the country may be considered as a part of the continent or of the sea. The wretched inhabitants take refuge on the sand-hills, or in little huts, which they construct on the summit of lofty stakes, whose elevation is conformable to that of the highest tides. When the sea rises, they appear like navigators; when it retires, they seem as though they had been shipwrecked. They subsist on the fish left by the refluent waters, and which they catch in nets formed of rushes or sea-weed. Neither tree nor shrub is visible on these shores. The drink of the people is rain-water, which they preserve with great care; their fuel, a sort of turf, which they gather and form with the hand. And yet these unfortunate beings dare to complain against their fate when they fall under the power and are incorporated with the empire of Rome."

develop the intellect, by narrowing the issues of controversy, than any of the other learned professions.* The success of early authorship did not allure him from its pursuit. After publishing, at the age of sixteen, a remarkable work on nautical navigation, he was enrolled as an advocate at the Hague. His practice increased until 1607. What rich experiences he hoarded in his conferences with his clients—the burgomasters of the city and the skippers of the sea; what diversions from close application, during this period of incessant preparation for his causes, and disquisitions on maritime law, were his, we have no means of knowing; for we have met with no record of his interior and office-life. But, doubtless, he here learned that solid sense, application and intimate knowledge of human nature which no imagination, however gorgeous, can supply; without which, learned pates are but prattling pedants, and official rank but the guinea's stamp, without the gold.

At this time he composed a work called *Mare Liberum*, in which he showed, from primary principles, that the sea was open

---

* No one can fail to remember the sarcasm which Burke flung at the legal profession. It has done the more injustice, because of its classic polish and distinguished source. In his speech on American taxation, he drew a masterly portrait of Grenville, but marred its fidelity by the peroration:—"He was bred to the law, a science which does more to quicken and invigorate the understanding than all the other kinds of learning put together. But it is not apt, except in persons very happily born, to open and liberalize the mind exactly in the same proportion." Had Burke practised the legal profession, the capital defect of his own master-mind might have been remedied. The response of the Earl of Rosslyn (then Solicitor General Wedderburn) to the above, would have lost its application and its sting. Referring to the practical knowledge of Grenville, and, by inuendo, to its want in Burke, he says: "Such were the disqualifications under which he was called to the first situation of administration, before it was understood that parts were spoiled by application, that ignorance was preferable to knowledge, and that any man of lively imagination, without practice in office, and without experience, might start up at once, a self-taught minister, and undertake the management of a great country amid difficult times." Jeffrey, Brougham, Eldon, and most of the American Presidents and Statesmen, and, above all, GROTIUS, are examples to refute the charge of illiberality. The ascendancy of lawyers—whom De Tocqueville calls the leaders of opinion in America—and the supply of the English peerage from the ranks of this profession, would sustain Wedderburn, unless, indeed, these have all been "very happily born."

to all, without distinction. The proof of such a principle now, would seem as superfluous as proving the existence of the sun; but at that time, when the Portuguese had portioned out all the Indian seas and the coast of Africa, below a certain parallel of latitude; and Spain had obtained from the Pontiff, Alexander the Sixth, the right to the rest of the ocean, lying in this Western world, it was a matter of some moment to the Netherlands that such exclusive pretensions should be broken down. In the settlement of the recent fishery difficulties between Great Britain and the United States, it may become necessary to recur to the venerable authority of Grotius, in this regard.

Grotius was a disciple of Arminius. He had imbibed his religious tenets from a clergyman named Uitenbogaard, with whom he had been early associated. He had also been associated in close friendship with the greatest man of Holland—BARNEVELDT; great in every act of his beneficent and spotless life; greater in that death, which made him the martyr of his country and liberty; greatest in the faith which he had learned from a greater than Arminius. Barneveldt was a child of the people. He became their Rienzi. Trade and wealth had given to the citizens such dignity and importance, that even the nobility sought to be enrolled in the guilds of traffic,—to become brewers and blacksmiths,—that they might attain preferment and rank. Barneveldt was the friend of the class from which he sprung, and of justice. Could he be less than the dearest friend of Grotius? He had leaned upon Grotius for counsel and succor in the early struggles against Philip. Fierce disputes between Francis Gomer, a harsh and bigoted zealot of the predestinarian stamp, and James Arminius, a meek and gentle soldier of the cross— whose character, open to the grace of heaven and conscious of its free will, gave hue to his tenets—began in the college of Leyden, where the contestants were professors. We may readily believe, to which party Barneveldt and Grotius would incline. It was just as natural that they should choose the temperance and toleration of Arminius, as that the cold-blooded Maurice, Prince of Orange, and his congenial ally, James I. of England, should incline toward the arrogant bigotry of Gomer. It is a mournful sight, to see Protestantism thus arrayed against itself; but we must remember, that Roger Williams and Lord Calvert had not then legislated, and that toleration was looked upon as humiliating submission, not heroic charity!

A decree against the Gomerists, with which Grotius was concerned, became obnoxious. The ambitious Prince of Orange fed the flames of discord, that he might attain power and humble Barneveldt. These feuds led to the death of Barneveldt, and to the imprisonment of Grotius. The latter was arrested for exciting an insurrection at Utrecht, to oppose the unlawful march of the Prince. After a long trial, he was incarcerated in a fortress near Gorcum, in South Holland, upon an island formed at the junction of the Waal and Meuse.

Imprisonment is but the restraint of the body. Those feel it most, whose minds have been fettered during their previous lives. Those feel it least who, in their solitude, can image great thoughts to vivify the future and to bless the race. A Socrates in confinement shows the world how to die for Truth, while he draws around his spirit the robe of immortality. A Baxter in prison—is he not reposing in that sainted rest, where " love is both work and wages ? " A Kossuth in exile—is he not pluming his wing for the loftiest flights of oratory, that he may sweep through the region of history, to give power and dignity to popular conscience? God has suffered many a sullen stone which confined the body, to preach to the souls of thousands. The chains, the racks and the dungeons of persecution, have tried in vain to stifle some of the noblest theories in science, and the holiest truths of religion.

" Wine issues from the trodden grape,
Iron's blister'd into steel."

The quaking jailor often starts to find at the unbarred door of the prisoner, the angels in white raiment appear, to bear away spiritual beauty and persuasive truth upon their wings, as healing for the nations! And, think you, an intellect so rarely endowed as Grotius, could be imprisoned in the Castle of Louvestein, yet leave no testimony?

Occupying part of his time in legal studies, he also found time to publish a critical examination of the Sermon on the Mount, and to write a treatise on the Truth of the Christian Religion. This latter work, which was somewhat on the plan of Paley, received translation into eight languages,—an evidence of the cosmopolitan nature of the mind which conceived the treatise on International Law.

It is not my purpose to examine his theological works. Whatever may be said of the faith of Arminius and Grotius, we know that illiberality was not one of its articles. If there is one virtue more Christ-like than another, it is that universal love of right and equality, which feels no physical boundary, and knows no difference between one people and another; and if there be one office more worthy than another of an humble worshipper of the Saviour, it is that of a law-giver, who draws from the conscience, from customs and from the Word of Life, the principles of peace on earth and good will to men, and binds them in a code which nations would be bound to obey. In this exalted office and with this primal virtue, even from the bars of the prison, the sovereign mind of the scholar ministered to the exigencies of his age, and formed about him a glorious court, where hourly he conversed with sages and philosophers, and, sometimes for variety, conferred with kings and emperors:

————————" and weighed their counsels,
Calling their victories, if unjustly got,
Unto a strict account; and, in his fancy,
Displaced their ill-placed statues."*

Grotius was enabled to escape, after two years' imprisonment, by the aid of his shrewd and devoted wife, who had him, at the risk of his life, let down from a window of the fortress, in the chest in which she was accustomed to have conveyed to him his books and linen. The soldiers who had guarded him, ignorant of their precious charge, removed the chest, while the wife remained

---

* Beaumont and Fletcher's Elder Brother.

trembling, lest he should be suffocated or dropped overboard, upon his passage across from the castle to Gorcum. He went to Paris, where he was naturalized by Louis XIII.; another link in that series of circumstances which Providence seems to have planned by which to denationalize him, the better to fit him for his great international labors. In 1625, he completed and gave to the world the crowning work of his life, "De Jure Belli et Pacis," the key-stone which locked in an arch of vigorous unity, the immense industry and learning of his life!

He remained in Paris, as the Embassador of Sweden, honored by all, until 1645. He then left for Sweden, where he remained long enough to receive the gratitude of the Queen; when he departed for his native land. He returned to the Lowlands with no stoical indifference; neither returned he like a tattered prodigal, in dishonor; neither came he back like a Coriolanus, with legions to avenge his wrongs. Like Dante at Ravenna, the glory of his compositions had, in some measure, reconciled him to banishment,—and his country, like Dante's native Florence, learned too late the value of the ornament it had lost; but unlike Florence, it was not compelled to entreat for the remains of the exile. The wreath of national fame had scarcely been enwarped for his brow, before his spirit fled to its Great Lawgiver. It was not permitted that land, which had imprisoned and exiled her noblest son, to compensate for such indignities by honoring Grotius *living*. He died shortly after he landed, and his body was taken to the tomb of his ancestors at Delft, where a fitting monument now points out to the traveler his place of repose.

But his spirit knows no repose. Ceaseless as the airy servitors of thought, it wings its way in maxim, in logic, in precedents, in treaties, and in ethical sanctions from age to age—establishing the rights of peace, arbitrating the quarrels of rulers, and staying the carnage of war. His spirit will never repose, so long as the independency of nations exists, and there is a necessity for reciprocal intercourse; so long as " justice is the great standing policy of civil society, and any eminent departure from it, under any circumstances, lies under the suspicion of being no policy at all;"* so long as the iniquitous maxim of Euphemus requires condemnation, "that there is nothing unjust that is profitable;"† and so long as there is a man who will not say, in the spirit of Antoninus, "*Civitas et patria mihi est, ut Antonino Roma ; ut homini Mundus*"—"As I am Antoninus, Rome is my country—as I am a man, the world!"

It is not my purpose to give you a disquisition upon the law of nations, nor to examine, critically, the great work of Grotius. It will be enough, for the purpose of infusing a proper regard for the influence of scholarship on the progress and preservation of society, to recur briefly to these labors.

Before his time, there was no systematic law of nations. With the exception of a lost work of Aristotle, it is not known that any treatise of this nature existed among the Greeks. Rome could have had no such law ; for that policy which engrossed the world by destroying the independency of nations, would forbid such a system. True, the fountains of justice have in all ages leaped upward in the human heart, and these have been well called the sources whence all civil laws are derived ; but not until the light of reformed Christianity shone, did the bow of promise bend over those fountains, as the sign of a better covenant between the nations. When Grotius began his labor, he found few precedents arising from contemporaneous history. The streams of morality had not only been tinctured, but poisoned by the bad faith of the reigning princes. The tyranny of Philip II., and his savage viceroy, the Duke of Alva, and their Inquisitors in Holland, and the total disregard of all principles of comity between Protestant and Catholic powers, except such as self-interest dictated, were not calculated to foster the growth of a law founded upon exact justice. Rude and undigested materials for the science were scattered over ancient history, and Grotius drew from them testimonies to strengthen his ethics and give sanction to his precepts.

It may seem strange, to one unacquainted with the sources of this law, which is a supreme, invariable, and uncontrollable rule

---

* Burke. † Thucydides.

of conduct to all men, that Grotius quotes so prodigally from the poets and orators of the past. But if it be true, that every poet and orator is in sympathy with his kind, and seldom utters sentiments at war with the best feelings of the heart, then morality is as well educible from the tragedies of Sophocles and Shakspeare, the comedies of Sheridan and Moliere, the fictions of Dickens and Le Sage, and the orations of Pericles and Burke, as from the ethics of Plato or the philosophy of Paley. The profuse erudition with which Grotius adorns and illustrates his principles, does not weaken them. He does not allow the authors of the past to speak for him, but with him. The dry details of science are thus relieved by the company of great spirits, whose genius forms a common tribute to the harmony of man and the stability of justice. Beautifully is the charm of such associations thus expressed: "Even Virtue and Wisdom themselves acquire new majesty in my eyes, when I thus see all the great masters of thinking and writing called together from all times and countries to do them homage, and to appear in their train!" Is it not a master intellect which thus gives to each thinker an influence unintended by himself, and directs his unconscious speech into such a channel as makes him a legislator for the world? Grotius does the same for us, when he makes each expression of truth and throb of conscience a clause in the great act preservative of human society.

One of the most thorough students and writers upon international law says of Grotius, that he produced a work which is, perhaps, the most complete that the world has yet owed, at so early a stage in the progress of any science, to the genius and learning of one man.*

He was deeply penetrated with the system of the Roman law, and its moral reason; well skilled in maritime law, an historian, a poet, a theologian, and a philosopher,—with a heart of singular amiability toward men and confidence in Providence, even in the harshest trials of life. To no one could be better committed the

---

* McIntosh's first Lecture on the Law of Nature and Nations.

duty of tracing the laws of nations to their sources, amidst the rugged sinuosities of Nature and the smiling fields of culture.

The mode in which he constructed the work, was not so convenient and orderly as science now demands. But the elements which Wolfe afterwards expanded, which Puffendorf enlarged, and which the comprehensive Vattel and our own perspicuous Wheaton reduced to system and authority, were there in their integrity. What Addison says of Architecture, may be applied to these several works of international law : " Greatness may be considered as relating to the bulk and body of the structure, as well as to the manner in which it is built." The walls of Babylon—its hanging gardens—its temple to Jupiter Belus, that rose a mile high by eight several stories, each story a furlong in height, and on the top of which was the Babylonian Observatory, are examples of the glory which springs from bulk and body— so gigantic as to put to shame our age of steam and invention, even in its greatest forces. The Pantheon, with its elegant proportion—its concave filling the entranced eye at once—and supported on graceful entablature and pillars, with its dome open to the pure light of an Italian heaven, is an example of greatness of manner at once uncommon and beautiful. The work of Grotius, like the former, depends most for its attraction upon the greatness of its bulk and body, its blooming gardens of literature, its temple of Justice, rising upward, story above story, and crowned with an eternal sunshine,—all giving evidence of a labor and genius which no subsequent age has dared to emulate. Wolfe and Puffendorf wandered amidst its labyrinths by the clue of Reason, and gazed from its towers with the eye of Faith. It was reserved for Vattel and Wheaton to re-construct out of its loose fragments the Pantheon of this science, and flood its shrines with the radiance of a more modern Reason. These authors have none of those redundancies of illustration and ornament which belong to Grotius, and which, in the morning of the science, were necessary to attract; but which now, owing to the progressive influence of thought, are no longer needed. Such redundancies would now divide and scatter the angles of light into a multitude of rays, and produce confusion. Since Grotius wrote, there has been infused into science greater precision of expression. We have more light upon social duty. The agitation and subsidence of international difficulties—the discoveries of countries before unknown—the policy of European intervention, and the "Holy Alliances" of a few great monarchs, for the control of lesser powers—the recent changes which steam and lightning have made in intercourse—the additional facilities for killing men, blowing up vessels, bombarding cities and attacking forts—and the ever-increasing spirit of humanity, generated by commerce and Christianity;—all these have, since Grotius wrote, changed somewhat the illustrations and precedents—the structure—though not at all shaken the eternal fundamental principles of international law!

How many important points of public law have since been contested by artillery and argument! The proposition which Grotius first laid down, and which seemed most difficult to establish, was the reverse of the old Roman maxim, *Inter arma leges silent;* for Grotius gave laws even to war! The right to reduce prisoners to slavery had not then met with denial. Ransom was expected and given as a private bargain. Exchange of prisoners was not known. The great question of "free ships, free goods; enemies' ships, enemies' goods," was not settled until the peace of Utrecht. The rights of blockade, since exercised by England upon the coast of France, so obnoxiously, have since been fixed on permanent principles, by the "armed neutrality" which was begun by Russia in the time of her Empress Catherine. The right of search, so prolific in dispute, especially as once exercised in the Channel, by English cruisers, upon the ships of the Baltic, has been limited and confined; while the maritime arrogance of England has been signally checked by the independent attitude of the United States. The world is under deep obligation to our former distinguished Minister to France, Gen. Cass, for his timely interference in this matter, to prevent an alliance which would have hampered our trade, and compromised our dignity as an independent nation. This vaunted right has been reduced to its proper level, by his firmness. It became simply a right of visit; then, a right of approach, which is equivalent to no right at all. The principle is thus laid down: " Such a right of approach seems indispensable for the fair and discreet exercise of authority; and the use of it cannot be justly deemed indicative of any design to insult or injure those approached; or to impede lawful commerce. On the other hand, it is as clear that no ship is, under such circumstances, bound to lie to, or wait the approach of any other ship. Her right to the free use of the ocean is as perfect as that of any other ship. An entire equality is presumed to exist."* The question concerning the impressment of our naturalized citizens, though made the subject of special embassy, has gradually been settling itself through Reason. Our last war failed to settle it by arms. The able argument of Webster, in the Ashburton correspondence, has done more than all the guns of Lundy's Lane, the cotton bags of New Orleans, and the victories of our navy, to protect from seizure and death the thousands which the overgrown countries of the old world eject annually from their bosom, to mingle their destinies with our own.†

But when shall the pretended right of the powerful to intervene and crush the people of other nations struggling to be free, be expunged from the precedents of international law?

"Shall crime breed crime forever,
Strength aiding still the strong?"

But we should not judge of the merits of Grotius by after exigencies which he could not foresee. Exact science cannot be applied to political affairs. No one but the OMNISCIENT, who sees all events harmonized in great generic laws, can lay down,

---

* Fifth Vol. Webster's Works, 338.

† Since writing the above, I have seen an account of a case in Hanover, of an American naturalized citzen from Charleston, S. C., who was impressed into eight years' service of the King, on his return to Fatherland, notwithstanding he had his naturalization papers and national passport. Proper steps have been taken to release him. It should be done on *principle*.

immutably, principles for all time. What science can do to develop the law of human progress, has been done in France by M. Comte, and in England by John Stuart Mill. The generalizations from history have been connected with the laws of human nature; the operations of physical and psychological agents upon collective masses of mankind have been noted and systematized; and there has been formed, not a science of universal maxims, applicable to every state and society,—like Locke's Constitution of North Carolina, and some of the early French Constitutions,— but uniform laws, resulting from the circumstances of each case. And although these laws, certain indeed as those of astronomy, will not enable us to predict the history of society, like that of the celestial appearances, for thousands of years to come; yet, our knowledge may be sufficient for practical guidance, if not for prophecy.* The causes and effects which the international jurist considers, are as minute as they are multiplied, subtle as complicated,—never the same, ever changing; nay, the same general truths, applicable to all the world, are, as Bacon has said, like waters, which do "take tinctures and tastes from the soils through which they run." Benefits incalculable flow to one nation, at one time, from one combination. Mischiefs the most tremendous whelm another, at another time, by another combination. Law, like the human body, though a system of beauty and proportion, is flexible; and like the human soul, it is plastic, in order to be progressive. It must not be fixed in the past, and deferential to forms. What a noble field is here for the influence of the scientific scholar! In this field Grotius labored. In this field American mind will reap its richest harvests in the next century. Here it may meet the exigencies of Time; make America a communicative light to the nations, and lead man in that path where restraint shall be unfelt in security, and security shall go hand in hand with liberty.

Security is obtained to human rights by the distribution of political power among the many, who are responsible; and not

---

* Mill's System of Logic—chapter on Social Science, page 549.

by its concentration among the irresponsible few. Absolute liberty is the absence of all restraint, consequently cannot exist even in a state of nature. The nearest approach to perfect liberty is had in society and in government, because "men are restrained in fewer actions by government, than they would be by violence without government." But since power has an innate tendency to aggrandize itself, it not only becomes necessary to protect man against his fellow by government, but man against the encroachment of government itself. How this latter can best be done, is the great question which the American Revolution answered. That response was communicated to the first French Revolution, and has ever since been agitating Europe. The parties of the world are on this point every where divided: Shall there be an increase or limitation of the powers of the ruler? The United States furnish the nearest approach to that system in which security and liberty are one; for here the powers are limited by a periodical return of the rulers among the ruled. The interests of both are most nearly identified. This is that civil refinement which we would have communicated to the nations. When we see a people spontaneously moving with this purpose, international law permits us to step beyond the pale of national boundary, to say: "*All hail, Republican sister! welcome within the great family of nations.*" Our diplomacy has not hid this magnificent truth under words. Webster has written it in plain and dignified language. Chevalier Hulsemann has read it, and sent and followed it home to the Hapsburg despot. The magical prosperity of our nation under our form of government, and the desire for happiness, give emphasis to our tone.* That tone is

---

* In illustration of this idea, let me quote from a paper written by an Apostle of Despotism in 1818, while the South American Republics were struggling to be free from Spain. Its author, the Archbishop of Malines, in speaking of these revolutions, says, that "the cause of kings and hierarchies of Europe is at stake. We must not conceal the embarrassments which will be caused in the bosom of Europe by the facilities, as it were, the open roads through which every one may now attain that education which was not long since in the possession of certain classes. Duty and personal feeling induce us to point out the dangers which

unambiguous. Do we not teach that individual and national morality is the same?—That the same rules which hold together men in families, and which form families into commonwealths, also link commonwealths as members of the great society of mankind?—That the rules which control and restrain injury—which regulate and augment benefits among men, ought to be applied to nations, for their well-being? True, nations acknowledge no head. They have no great Congress, or visible ruler. They are, nominally, independent. But it is no less true, that God never made an independent man, than an independent nation. Individuals are no less dependent on their neighbors, and bound to exercise toward them justice, honesty, and humanity, than are nations. This is the noblest view which human law can take of human affairs. This is that law whose seat is in the bosom of God—whose voice is the collected wisdom and the harmony of the world—the mother of peace and joy. This is that justice of which Grotius speaks when he says, that "it is approved of even as injustice is condemned by the consent of all good men; yea, and what is the greatest comfort, the one hath God for its Avenger, and the other God for its Patron; who so reserves his judgments after this life, that he ofttimes gives a taste of them even in this."

This higher, nay highest law, has been broken—never broken to aid, but always to oppress the people—so shamefully within

---

arise from the prolonged struggle between Spain and America, and the facility which is given to the last to dispose of its fate. We are the more drawn to this observation, because in the number of American Constitutions which we have seen, we have not met with one which included a single word referring to royalty. On the contrary, all are struck with a deep dye of republicanism, and lean more to the institutions of the United States than those of Europe. *The danger is so much the greater, as no nation equals in prosperity the United States. There is a great attraction in the view of happiness; and the nature of man leads him to seek it and make it his own.*" (*Niles' Reg.*, vol. 14, p. 311.) Ah! this in 1818. Now, in 1852, has the danger decreased, by our unequaled prosperity since? Has happiness ceased to attract? or men become lovers of misery, under royalty? Just think of that, in connection with the thirty thousand emigrants who land monthly at New York!

the last century and the last few years, by the great powers of Europe, that it has seemed but a plaything to be used or thrown away, as it suited the caprice and interest of kings and princes. The wanton spoliation of Poland, on the 5th of August, 1772,— in which Frederick of Prussia and Catharine of Russia took part, and the amiable house of Hapsburg was not too scrupulous, even then, to join,—was a piece of magnificent scoundrelism, which neither Nicholas nor Joseph, with all their endeavors to rival their ancestors and grind Hungary into her ensanguined dust, have been able to excel. Determined that this act should shine out in nefarious conspicuousness, a diet of the aggressive powers undertook to apologize to the world,—for the world's conscience had been tortured by the accursed international larceny; and what reasons were given? (1) Because Poland had a constitution defective on account of its——republicanism; (2) because the harmony of the surrounding powers might not be disturbed by——free thoughts; (3) and in order to fix permanently the boundaries of Poland, they——should be entirely taken away! And this was done by the powers which afterwards complained of France for her aggrandizing republicanism. This triple alliance continued to exercise its encroachments until the French Revolution. Its humiliation came, when one of the children of that revolution, Bonaparte, thundered around Vienna, and made Moscow a charred ruin. Oh! that the present Bonaparte might prove a NAPOLEON, to make these arrogant thrones tremble before the power of the people!

The Holy Alliance was the same affiliation, under another form. Its formation is the most interesting fact in modern history. It was signed at Paris by Francis, William and Alexander, on the 16th day of September, 1815, while the allied armies were practising in the Champs Elysèe, and the Cossacks were bivouacking in the Boulevards. After appealing to God, their conscience, and the rules of private morality for their public conduct, these royal Pharisees "bound themselves in confraternity, regarding themselves as members of one family, to lend to each other, on *every occasion and in every place*, assistance and succor." Well have they kept their bond. They said to the Neapolitan people, in the revolution of 1820, "receive whom we appoint over you!" Austria said the same to Piedmont in 1821; and France, in 1822, to Spain. At Laybach and Troppau they met again, to stop the progress of pernicious democracy; but we are especially indebted to the secret treaty at Verona, in 1822, for the monstrous conspiracy in all its magnitude. The first article of the treaty reveals the vital sympathy upon which these Powers have subsequently acted. It reads as follows: "That the high contracting parties, convinced that the principles of representative government are equally inconsistent with monarchical principles, as is the doctrine of popular sovereignty with divine right, pledge themselves mutually to each other, in the most solemn manner, to exert all their efforts to annihilate representative government, in all countries in Europe in which it may exist, and to prevent its introduction in states where it is now unknown."

In 1849, Russia carried out the contract—how faithfully—toward Hungary; and France (*et tu Brute?*) acted in the same spirit toward the high-souled Mazzini and his compatriots, when the Janiculum hill ran with the blood of the young Romans; the marble halls of the Vatican resounded with the cannonade of Oudinot, and the old walls gave way to the crusade for martial tyranny against popular liberty!

In neither of these, did Great Britain concur. She stood, too, by the United States against this Holy Alliance, when it undertook to interfere between Spain and her American colonies. We then protested that nations were independent; that they were the judges of their own form of government, and that republicanism should not be crushed by king-craft—at least upon this Western Continent, its last, best refuge. We said: "Your Nesselrodes and Metternichs have solemnly appealed to the Christian's God, and have hypocritically called the solemn sanctions of conscience and justice to your aid; but we will not forget who sacrificed Poland to Russia, Saxony to Prussia, the ancient Republics of Genoa and Venice to Sardinia and Austria." This alliance of perdition still exists. Even as I write, the festal garlands are not withered which decorated the palatial halls of Berlin and Vienna, to welcome the Russian Czar to these seats of illy-gotten and worse-used power. A recent telegraph, has flashed the fact forth that the Five Powers have called on the Federal Government of Switzerland to recognize the right of Prussia to Neufchatel! The free mountain air of Republicanism must be confined in the stifling caves of Despotism; and the sisterhood of Swiss is to be severed—because the *Powers* say so. I hope the Swiss will resist this arrogance of the five royal *bullies*, with the spirit of Tell and the olden time. The arch perjurer of Naples, scorned by the world for his cruelty and crime, still sits in his palace, overlooking a bay of jeweled beauty, a prisoner afraid to mingle with the people he rules. Inhumanity, defying the law of nations and of God, plays its royal game in that old seat of luxury and ease. Has it no fear of the retributive fate of Pompeii? As sure as God writes all history, there is for crime, whether kingly or beggarly, retribution. Well do I remember the force with which this truth was impressed on my mind, upon a godless Sunday, in Versailles. The Bourbon palaces of the Trianon were tenantless, or guarded by a few soldiers of the Republic, over whose sentry-march, the words " Liberté, Egalité et Fraternitè," spoke—*retribution!* The great halls of Louis XIV., tapestried with the richness of the Gobbelins—once the proud palace wherein Racine, Corneillé and Voltaire did homage to the Grand Monarch—echoed the curious tread of the stranger, whose whispering inquiries gave back the solemn response—*retribution.* The walls yet blazed with the canvas upon which David and other artists had expressed, in life-like colors, the glories of Napoleon and his battle-fields, and eager thousands of volatile French gazed upon them, transported as with religion; but these glories spoke of an instrumentality used by Providence for—*retribution.* There was one room, where glittered in gold the coach of state that once belonged to Charles X., the last of the elder Bourbons who had ruled here. It had once rolled around those musical fountains and down those leafy avenues. That empty show spoke—*retribution.* Another chamber was dedicated to paintings illustrative of the younger branch of the Bourbons. There Louis Philippe had commanded art to immortalize his sons, for their gallantry at San Juan d'Ulloa and Algiers; but the crayon sketch, and the half-finished coloring,—these mere skeletons of glory,—spoke of —*retribution*. The revolution of 1848, had overtaken both monarch and artist, and both hastened from a people's vengeance. Painfully impressive was the fate of that old monarch, pictured in those unfinished embellishments. He died a wanderer from the people who had elevated him, and whom he had betrayed. He went down like a bark in a starless night, amid the storms of mid ocean, "with scarce a pitying eye to weep his fall, or a friendly hand to record his struggle."

Since that time, a common fellowship has united the monarchs of Europe; and while thus cementing, the United States have visited the Golden Horn, received from the hands of the Mahommedan, and conducted to our shores, by the sanction of international law, a thinker and scholar—untitled and exiled—with "no starry breast or coroneted brow," but with a breast of sympathy and a brow of genius, the chosen champion of European freedom —LOUIS KOSSUTH! He has received the acclaim and the aid of well-wishing millions; he has plead before the tribunal of popular conscience, the justice of the cause of Hungary, as tried by the law of nations. He will return to England. There he will meet the noble Joseph Mazzini. The people will know their own. Bayonets are yet arrayed against Reason—Reason must provide herself with bayonets; *then God help the right!* Great as is the calamity of war, (thanks to Grotius, whom I would not forget, who has mitigated its severity by constructing a code of humanity out of the very passions of men,) let that war come! welcome its alarms, its carnage! France and the United States, perhaps phlegmatic Britain aiding, may yet beat back the crusading Cossack; the sun may sink in blood, but by and by there will be a sunrise of beauty. The trophy will be constitutional freedom, and the independence of nations! In that war, have we no part? Has the scholar and writer no weapon—no service? Abstract truth is the scholar's weapon; it is the revolutionary principle of all time. The social system is moulded by its viewless agency! What magic was there in Harrington, that Cromwell should tremble at his Imaginary Commonwealth?—what in the unpublished writings of Sydney, that a Stuart should fear for his crown?—what in Montesquieu and Locke, that old systems of government should be reviewed in the light of their science, and the grand principles of toleration observed? Who so passive as not to be moved under the power of the pen—that wand of fairy potency—whether in the hand of Rousseau, disturbing the prejudices of ages, and rocking the social structure by his gesture; or in the hand of Burke, calming the volcanic throes of society; or in the hand of Adam Smith, regulating trade and establishing the principles of interchange?—at all times, establishing the principle, for which Sydney was condemned and executed, as false in the common law of England, as it is true in the law of mind and of nations,—*Scribere est agere:* WRITING IS ACTING! Words and thoughts are above national laws, as the Creator is above the created. International law, especially, springs from them; for it is the offspring of opinion. It is the conscience of the world: it depends for its force on the sanctions of morality. The thinker and scholar are the holy lights ever burning upon the altar of conscience. How ennobling the thought, gentlemen, that you and I—the humblest of us—by the right of our common reason, may become members of this great congress of opinion;—may give our breath of enthusiasm, our word of caution, our ideas of duty, our hopes of human progress; and blend them with the common voice, which is as powerful to condemn as it is glorious to reward! Heedless of storm, defying ocean-boundaries, subtle as the electric fluid, your influence may be felt forming that public opinion whose protests, if not at once heeded, forbid at least the degrading idea of acquiescence, and which arrays before impartial history those heinous acts, whose fraud is not lessened by its splendor!

GENTLEMEN OF THE ATHENIAN SOCIETY: In conclusion, allow me to address you, whose partiality has invited me hither, with especial reference to the subject of International Law. It is yours thus to conserve justice and advance your race. Devote the highest exertions of your mind to spread such a beneficent enthusiasm among men. You have a country as varied in its surface as it is rich in its resources; girdled by a sea-coast over five thousand miles in length, and an area of territory which has increased since your confederation from 800,000 square miles to nearly 3,000,000, upon which now 25,000,000 of souls live—all accessible to your speech. By virtue of your scholarship, you are contemporary with Plato and Thucydides; you may lash luxury with Juvenal, hurl philippics with Demosthenes, indulge sarcasm with Erasmus, and brand political profligacy with Junius. The spirits of the gifted, by night and by day, gather around you as they did around Grotius, bidding you treasure up their thoughts for the weal of man and the honor of God!

America must be the theatre of international thought. As all the nations are sending their sons here to learn of us, so will react upon them our example and our ideas. Make them great, good and glorious! The world will be yours to enter soon. Oh! march not through it with the pulseless heart, the languid eye, and to the muffled drum of cold conservatism, leaving no foot-prints in the sands of time. Look not upon humanity as a painted image, or an abstraction, but as a home—a glowing home—where immortal hopes circle, and from which they take wing for the upper air. This world is selfish, and prone to scorn the enthusiasm which advances, and by advancing, preserves; but its honors—they wither before the flowers are enwoven in the garland. Cultivate enthusiasm, not for its guerdon, but for its holy object. It is the perfume and life of the soul. There is a calm depth in the human soul, whose mirror answers to the beautiful and pure; whose margin is fringed with the groves of meditation, and whose reflection is—heaven. The passionate tumults of the world disturb it not; but the tiniest pebble, dropped by the hand of thoughtful enthusiasm, may form there its flotilla of wavelets, whose ever-widening circles kiss all the shore, and, in refluent beauty, meet to mingle with that clear mirror forever. Have you no influence, whether it be the unpolished pebble or the priceless pearl, wherewith to stir this crystalline depth? You have! answer to God for its use! Fix first the perceptions of duty to yourself, your country, and your kind; and, as you cannot love God too much, so neither, in their performance, put bounds to your enthusiasm. And if you would glow with an excellence kindred to that of Grotius, imbibe the spirit of the last words of his great work: " I pray that God, who alone can do it, may instil these things into the hearts of those who manage Christendom, giving them a mind thoroughly instructed in all rights, both human and divine; and that they always may remember, that Christianity was chosen of God, as his vicegerent on earth, to govern man, the best and most beloved of all his creatures.

ALL GLORY BE GIVEN TO GOD!"

Printed by Libri Plureos GmbH in Hamburg, Germany